NBA CHAMPIONSHIP:

2016

ALL-TIME LEADING SCORER:

LeBRON JAMES (2003–10, 2014–PRESENT):

20,868 POINTS

(AS OF APRIL 13, 2017)

THE NBA: A HISTORY OF HOOPS

CLEVELAND CAVALIERS

THE NBA: A HISTORY OF HOOPS

CLEVELAND CAVALIERS

BY JIM WHITING

CREATIVE EDUCATION CREATIVE PAPERBACKS

Published by Creative Education
and Creative Paperbacks

P.O. Box 227, Mankato, Minnesota 56002

Creative Education and Creative Paperbacks
are imprints of The Creative Company

www.thecreativecompany.us

Design and production by Blue Design

Printed in the United States of America

Photographs by Corbis (Bettmann), Getty Images
(Steve Babineau/NBA, Mark Blinch/Getty Images
Sport, Nathaniel S. Butler/NBA, Focus on Sport/
Getty Images Sport, Jesse D. Garrabrant/NBAE,
Jeff Goode/Toronto Star, David Liam Kyle/NBA,
Ronald Martinez/Getty Images Sport, Manny
Millan/Sports Illustrated, Greg Nelson/Sports
Illustrated, Nivek Neslo, Dick Raphael/NBA, Rogers
Photo Archive/Getty Images Sport, Gregory
Shamus/Getty Images Sport, Carl Skalak/Sports
Illustrated, Carl Skalak/Sports Illustrated Classic,
Tom Szczerbowski/Getty Images Sport, Tony
Tomsic/Sports Illustrated), Newscom (Mitchell
Layton/MCT, Ting Shen/Xinhua/Photoshot)

Library of Congress Cataloging-in-Publication Data

Names: Whiting, Jim, 1943- author.

Title: Cleveland Cavaliers / Jim Whiting.

Series: The NBA: A History of Hoops.

Includes bibliographical references and index.

Summary: This high-interest title summarizes the
history of the Cleveland Cavaliers professional
basketball team, highlighting memorable events
and noteworthy players such as LeBron James.

Identifiers: LCCN 2016046225 / ISBN 978-1-60818-
840-6 (hardcover) / ISBN 978-1-62832-443-3
(pbk) / ISBN 978-1-56660-888-6 (eBook)

Subjects: LCSH: 1. Cleveland Cavaliers
(Basketball team)—History—Juvenile
literature. 2. Cleveland Cavaliers (Basketball
team)—Biography—Juvenile literature.

Classification: LCC GV885.52.C57 W55 2017 /
DDC 796.323/640977132—dc23

CCSS: RI.4.1, 2, 3, 4; RI.5.1, 2, 4; RI.6.1, 2,
3; RF.4.3, 4; RF.5.3, 4; RH. 6-8. 4, 5, 7

First Edition HC 9 8 7 6 5 4 3 2 1

First Edition PBK 9 8 7 6 5 4 3 2 1

CONTENTS

A hub of transportation, CLEVELAND sits where the Cuyahoga River flows into Lake Erie.

CLEVELAND JOINS THE NBA

O n October 29, 2003, Cleveland's
Gund Arena shook with anticipation. LeBron James
was about to make his National Basketball Association
(NBA) debut with the Cleveland Cavaliers. James was

only 18. Less than a year before, he was playing high school basketball. Reporters had already nicknamed him "King James." The previous spring, he was the top choice in the NBA Draft. Before even playing an NBA game, James had signed a $90-million contract with Nike. Would he live up to all the hype? Hundreds of reporters were on hand. They came from as far away as Canada, Taiwan, and Japan. Adding to the pressure, James hadn't played well in nationally televised preseason games. Opposing players backed off and dared him to shoot. Most of the time he missed.

Now it was time for the real thing. "I was nervous," James said. "I couldn't sleep the night before." He couldn't even prepare properly. Photographers and TV cameramen stalked his every move during warm-ups. Barely a minute into the game, James passed

As 2004 Rookie of the Year, **LeBRON JAMES** made an instant impact on Cleveland.

HONESTY IS THE BEST POLICY

NICK MILETI, OWNER, 1970–80

Most NBA owners use their own money to buy teams. Nick Mileti used other people's money. It wasn't just the Cavaliers. He made many purchases this way. He convinced his investors that they were getting a good deal. "They knew I was honest. I had great parents, so it just isn't in my nature to cheat," Mileti said. It was in his nature to take risks. "In those days, everybody was leaving," he explained of his desire to have an NBA team. "I was betting my life on my hometown." The crowds who root for the Cavaliers today are glad he did.

to a teammate for a thundering dunk. Then, he scored his first NBA points on a jump shot. He went on to score 10 more points and had 3 assists, 2 rebounds, and 2 steals—in the first quarter. He finished with 25 points. The Cavaliers lost the game. But James was the game's leading scorer. His stat line included 9 assists, 6 rebounds, and 4 steals. "When we first entered the arena nobody knew exactly what LeBron was going to do," said Cleveland coach Paul Silas. "I thought he was going to be good, but not nearly as good as he was. It was unbelievable." Cleveland had never won an NBA title. After this game, fans began thinking that a championship banner might be within reach.

The NBA had expanded in February 1970. The league added Portland, Buffalo, and Cleveland. Cleveland wasn't an obvious choice. The city was going through hard times. Cleveland businessman Nick Mileti believed in its future. He raised enough money to buy the franchise. He had to work quickly. The NBA Draft was just six weeks away. The team didn't have a coach. It didn't even have a name. The Cleveland newspaper, *The Plain Dealer*, held a contest. More than 11,000 people responded with suggestions. Cleveland resident Jerry Tomko submitted the winning entry. It was Cavaliers, often shortened to Cavs. He wrote, "They represent a group of daring, fearless men, whose life's pact was never surrender, no matter what the odds." The team's first logo showed

The Cavaliers slowly improved until they reached the playoffs in 1975–76.

a swashbuckling cavalier. He looked like one of the Three Musketeers. He wore a floppy hat, cape, and high boots and carried a sword.

There wasn't much action in the first season. The team consisted of veterans other teams didn't want and a handful of untested rookies. Coach Bill Fitch was realistic about the team's chances. "Remember, my name is Fitch, not Houdini," he said. The Cavs lost their first 15 games. They edged fellow expansion team Portland by two points for their first victory. Then the Cavs dropped another 12 in a row. They finished 15–67. It was the league's worst record.

TASTING SUCCESS AND FAILURE

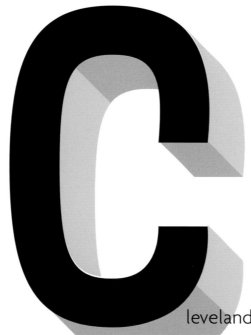

leveland had the first pick in the 1971 NBA Draft. It took 6-foot-4 shooting guard Austin Carr. He became the face of the team.

AUSTIN CARR spent 9 seasons in Cleveland, averaging 16.2 points per game.

An original Cavaliers player, BOBBY "BINGO" SMITH offered dependability to the team.

The Cavs won 23, 32, and 29 games the following three seasons. The losing records kept fans away. There was another problem. The team played its home games in Cleveland Arena. Built in 1937, the arena was outdated. Owner Nick Mileti built a new arena in Richfield in 1974. Many people criticized Mileti for the site. It was in the middle of a cornfield more than 20 miles from downtown Cleveland. But home attendance doubled at the new Richfield Coliseum. According to *Sports Illustrated*

LEGENDS OF THE HARDWOOD

THE MIRACLE OF RICHFIELD

NBA PLAYOFFS, FIRST ROUND, WASHINGTON VS. CLEVELAND, APRIL 13–29, 1976

The Bullets were heavily favored. That didn't matter to Cleveland fans. They were stoked about their team's first playoff appearance. "The fans would get rolling a half hour before the game," said Austin Carr. "They'd be stomping on the floor, 'Let's go, Cavs! Let's go, Cavs!' It was to the point where the entire building was shaking." The series was especially exciting because of how close the scores were. Two of the Cavs' first three victories were by a single point. Dick Snyder's jump shot with 4 seconds left in Game 7 gave Cleveland an 87–85 win. Fans rushed the floor and mobbed the players.

Sharpshooting guard came through in clutch situations.

magazine, "No arena was more beautiful than the Coliseum." The Cavs added sharpshooting guard Dick Snyder and towering forward Jim Chones. They helped Cleveland finish 40–42 in 1974–75. But Carr was out with a knee injury. The team missed the playoffs by just one game.

Cleveland added veteran shot blocker and rebounder Nate Thurmond the following season. The Cavs went 49–33. They qualified for the playoffs for the first time. Fitch did his best Houdini imitation in the first round. Cleveland defeated the Washington Bullets four games to three. The series became known as "the Miracle of Richfield." Newspaper reporter Burt Graeff wrote, "The place was a frenzy. Television announcers doing the national broadcast couldn't hear each other. Bill Fitch was trying to write down some last-minute instructions for the players, and the locker room blackboard was literally shaking. That season is when basketball in Cleveland was born." Unfortunately, Chones broke his foot in practice before the next round. Cleveland played hard against the Boston Celtics. But they lost the series, four games to two.

Fitch guided the Cavs to 43–39 records the following two seasons, but there were no more miracles. The Cavs were bounced in the first round of the playoffs both times. They stumbled to a 30–52 mark in 1978–79. Fitch quit. After another losing record, Mileti sold the team to Ted Stepien. The next three years were the low point of Cavaliers history. Stepien proved to be one of the worst owners in NBA history. Guard World B. Free was one of the few bright spots. He joined the team in 1982. He soon became the leading scorer. "World sincerely believes every shot he takes will go in," said fellow guard John Bagley. "A lot of times, he's right."

LEGENDS OF THE HARDWOOD

WORST NBA OWNER?

TED STEPIEN, OWNER, 1980–83

Owner Ted Stepien was a poor judge of talent. He traded high draft choices for marginal veterans. He tried to schedule "home games" in other states. He even made racist comments. Fans called the team the Cleveland Cadavers because they lost so many games. The *New York Times* said the Cavs were "the worst club and most poorly run franchise in professional basketball." When Stepien sold the team, the NBA realized his ownership had been a disaster. The league granted the Cavaliers extra first-round draft picks for four years. Now, the "Stepien Rule" forbids a team from trading its top draft choice two years in a row.

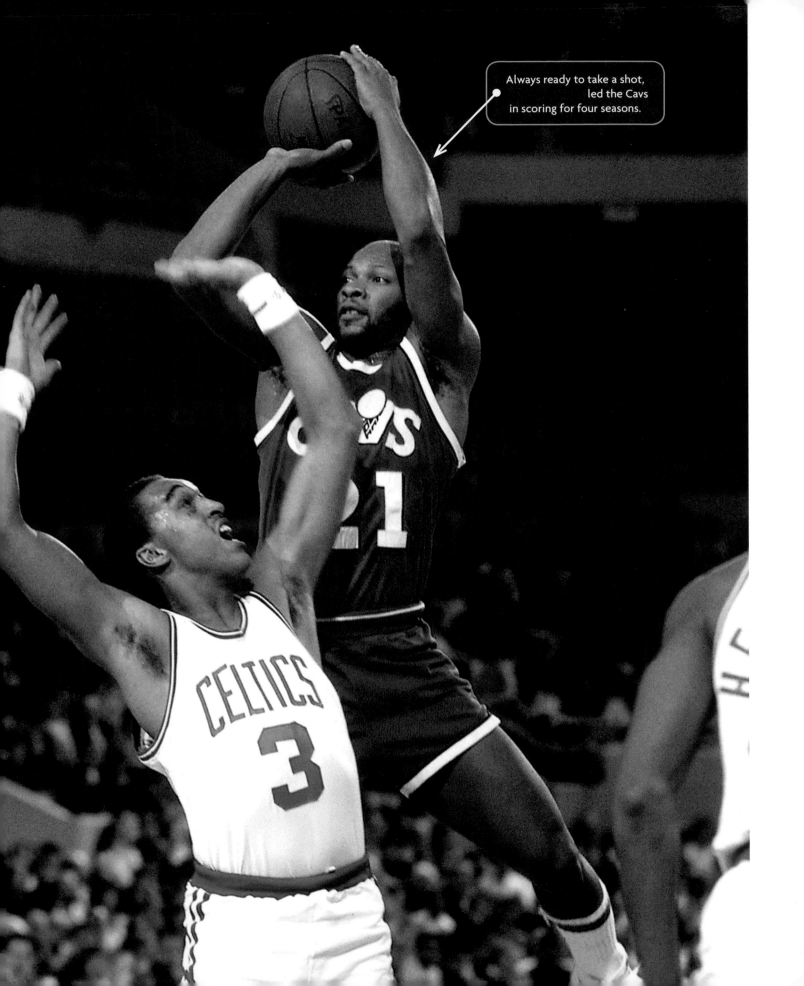

Always ready to take a shot, led the Cavs in scoring for four seasons.

"WORLD SINCERELY BELIEVES EVERY SHOT HE TAKES WILL GO IN," SAID FELLOW GUARD JOHN BAGLEY. "A LOT OF TIMES, HE'S RIGHT."

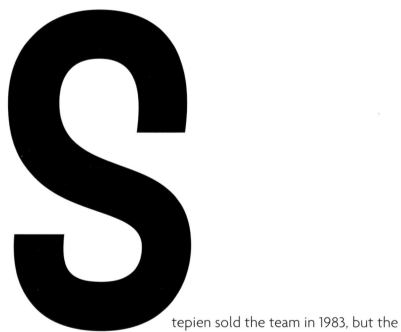

tepien sold the team in 1983, but the damage had been done. The Cavs had losing records for five years. They reached the playoffs in 1985 after starting 2–19. But they lost to Boston in the first round, three games to one. It was a heartbreaking series. All three losses were by three points or fewer. Free did his best, averaging more than 26 points a game.

REPAIRING THE DAMAGE

Under coach Lenny Wilkens, the Cavs finally had a winning season again in 1987–88, going 42–40. They had drafted 7-foot center Brad Daugherty and explosive guard Ron Harper the previous

Seven-foot center **BRAD DAUGHERTY** led Cleveland to the playoffs six times.

A quick release and perfect form made **MARK PRICE** one of the NBA's top shooters.

year. They added sharpshooting point guard Mark Price and long-limbed power forward Larry Nance. But Cleveland lost to Chicago in the first round of the playoffs. Everything meshed the following year. The Cavs went 57–25. It was their best record. Once again, they couldn't get past Chicago in the playoffs. Injuries and bad trades plagued the Cavs the next two seasons. They bounced back in 1991–92, winning 57 games. But they lost to the Bulls in the Eastern Conference finals, four games to two. When the Bulls bounced the Cavs from the playoffs yet again in 1992–93, Wilkens was done. "It's been a great seven years with the Cavaliers," he said. "However, I think it's time to move on." Defensive-

29

FROM HERO TO GOAT

GAME 5, EASTERN CONFERENCE PLAYOFFS, CLEVELAND VS. CHICAGO, MAY 7, 1989

Cleveland's Craig Ehlo had scored Cleveland's last eight points. His final basket gave the Cavs a 100–99 lead. Seconds remained. The Bulls' Michael Jordan went up for a jump shot. He suspended himself in midair long enough for Ehlo to sail past him. With one second left, he released the ball. It went in. Chicago won 101–100. The ESPN TV network called it the best play of Jordan's career. "If I hadn't been out of position I could have stopped that shot," Ehlo said later. "I had a hand in his face but only for a split second."

LEGENDS OF THE HARDWOOD

TRAVELING COURT

In 1997, tiny Grace Christian School in Staunton, Virginia, wanted its own basketball court. The school learned that the court and baskets of Richfield Coliseum (pictured) were available. A local contractor donated an empty warehouse. It would be the school's gym. A trucking company donated two big rigs to bring the floor to Virginia. The Cavs did their part. Another school offered more money. The Cavs stood by the original deal. Today the floor still displays the Cavs logo. It reminds the school's athletes of its heritage. "All the greats played on this floor," said girls' basketball coach Randall McNair.

minded Mike Fratello replaced him. "I'd rather win ugly than lose pretty," said the new coach. Ugly or not, the team kept winning for several more seasons. But Cleveland still made early playoff exits.

The Cavs missed out on a golden opportunity in the 1996 NBA Draft. They chose 6-foot-10 center Vitaly Potapenko. Nicknamed the "Ukraine Train," he lasted less than three seasons and averaged just 7 points a game. Cleveland fans watched the three selections right after Potapenko go on to superstardom. They were Kobe Bryant, Peja Stojaković, and Steve Nash. Both Bryant and Nash were named Most Valuable Player (MVP). Stojaković became an All-Star. A three-way trade brought power forward Shawn Kemp to Cleveland in 1997. He was a starter in the 1998 All-Star Game. The following year, he averaged more than 20 points a game. Soon, Fratello moved on. Without him, the team endured several losing seasons. Injuries, constant coaching changes, and roster turnover hounded the team. The Cavs of the early 2000s often appeared to be playing street ball. They sported flashy style but lacked teamwork.

KING JAMES REIGNS

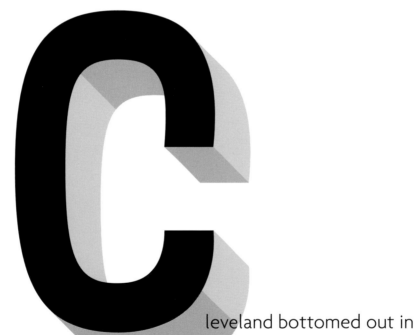

Cleveland bottomed out in 2002–03 with a 17–65 record. It was the team's worst mark in 21 years. The dismal showing gave the Cavs the first pick in the 2003 NBA Draft. There was no question about whom they would choose: LeBron James. James

Averaging 30 points per game in 2007–08, LEBRON JAMES topped the league in scoring.

As of 2016, JAMES had earned All-Star status eight times while with the Cavs.

34

had played high school ball in nearby Akron. He led his team to three state championships. He was on the cover of *Sports Illustrated*. Twice he was named Gatorade National Player of the Year.

James lived up to the hype. He scored 25 points in his first game. "I thought he was going to be good, but not nearly as good as he was," said coach Paul Silas. "It was unbelievable." Later that season, he became the youngest player in NBA history to score at least 40 points in a game. He was just the third rookie to average at least 20 points, 5 rebounds, and 5 assists. Not surprisingly, he was selected Rookie of the Year. He helped Cleveland win 35 games, doubling its record from the year before. In the previous season, average attendance was 11,497. It rose to 18,288 in James's first season. James was even better in 2004–05. He averaged 27.2 points, 7.4 rebounds, 7.2 assists, and 2.2 steals per game. He became the youngest player named to the All-NBA team. Cleveland narrowly missed the playoffs, finishing 42–40.

In Cleveland from 2008 to 2010, MO WILLIAMS returned for the title-winning season.

> "WE BELIEVE IT WILL BE A GOLDEN ERA OF BASKETBALL FOR THE FANS AND COMMUNITY OF THIS HARDWORKING AND WELL-DESERVING TOWN."

Quicken Loans founder Dan Gilbert bought the team before the 2005–06 season. "We believe it will be a golden era of basketball for the fans and community of this hardworking and well-deserving town," he said. That "golden era" got off to a good start. The Cavs won 50 games. The first round of the playoffs echoed the Miracle of Richfield. Cleveland beat the Washington Wizards by a point in two overtime games to win the series 4–2. But it lost to Detroit in the next round. In 2006–07, the Cavs played in the NBA Finals for the first time. But San Antonio was too tough. The Spurs swept the series. Cleveland advanced to the conference semifinals the following year. Boston bounced them out. James had a sensational season in 2008–09. He averaged 28.4 points, 7.6 rebounds, and 7.2 assists per game. He was also runner-up for Defensive Player of the Year. He earned his first MVP award. Plus, he led the team to a franchise-record 66 wins. Another key to success was point guard Mo Williams. The Cavs swept both Detroit and Atlanta in the playoffs. But Cleveland lost the Eastern Conference finals to Orlando. James repeated as MVP the following year. But when the Cavs lost in the conference semifinals, James was booed.

fired up Cleveland fans with his ritualistic pregame "chalk toss."

BREAKING—AND MENDING—A CITY'S HEART

In 2010, James became a free agent. That meant he could sign with any team. He announced his choice in a TV show called *The Decision*. The program

40

LeBRON JAMES: NFL STAR?

LeBRON JAMES, FORWARD, 6-FOOT-8, 2003–10, 2014–PRESENT

LeBron James played wide receiver for his high school football team for two years. Ohio State and Notre Dame wanted him to play football for them. Some people even think he could play in the National Football League (NFL). "He's a 6-foot-8, 250-pound freak of stature," wrote ESPN's Tim Graham. "He would tower above NFL defensive backs and other receivers." Players such as Green Bay safety Mark Murphy agreed. "I felt like that was one kid that could have gone from high school to the NFL," he said. James even made a brief appearance in the *Madden NFL 12* video game.

LEGENDS OF THE HARDWOOD

raised $6 million for charity. But there was no charity for Cleveland fans. James said he was joining the Miami Heat. Moments later, he became one of the most disliked athletes in the country. Cleveland exploded. Gilbert published an open letter criticizing James. Fans burned his jersey.

ithout James, the Cavs scraped together just 19 wins in the 2010–11 season. Cleveland traded Williams to the Los Angeles Clippers for guard Baron Davis. Davis played the final 15 games of the season before being released. However, the Cavs struck gold in the NBA Draft for the second time in less than a decade. The Williams trade gave them the top overall pick. With it, Cleveland chose point guard Kyrie Irving. Irving became an instant sensation. He averaged 18.5 points and 5.4 assists per game. He was named Rookie of the Year. Despite his accomplishments, Cleveland still struggled. The team won just 21 games in the strike-shortened

2011–12 season, then 24 and 33 the following two seasons.

Everything changed on July 11, 2014. Two weeks earlier, LeBron James once again had become a free agent. Where would he go this time? An article in *Sports Illustrated* provided the answer. "When I left Cleveland, I was on a mission," James said. "I was seeking championships, and we won two. But Miami already knew that feeling. Our city [Cleveland] hasn't had that feeling in a long, long, long time. My goal is still to win as many titles as possible, no question. But what's most important for me is bringing one trophy back to Northeast Ohio." Fans immediately forgave him for leaving four years earlier. As a bonus, James persuaded big man Kevin Love to join him in Cleveland. With Irving, the team could now boast a Big Three. Swingman Tristan Thompson added strength from the bench. Cleveland roared to a 53–29 record in the regular season. The Cavs swept both Boston and Atlanta in the playoffs. They blasted into the 2015 NBA Finals. But the Golden State Warriors were just too tough. The Warriors won the series four games to two.

Mo Williams returned to the Cavs at the start of the 2015–16 season. In a way, that meant Cleveland got Irving ... for free. With 57 wins, the Cavs charged into the playoffs. Easy series wins over Detroit, Atlanta, and Toronto propelled them into the NBA Finals. "I came back for a reason," James said after the Cavs knocked off the Warriors. "I came back to bring a championship to our city. I knew what I was capable of doing."

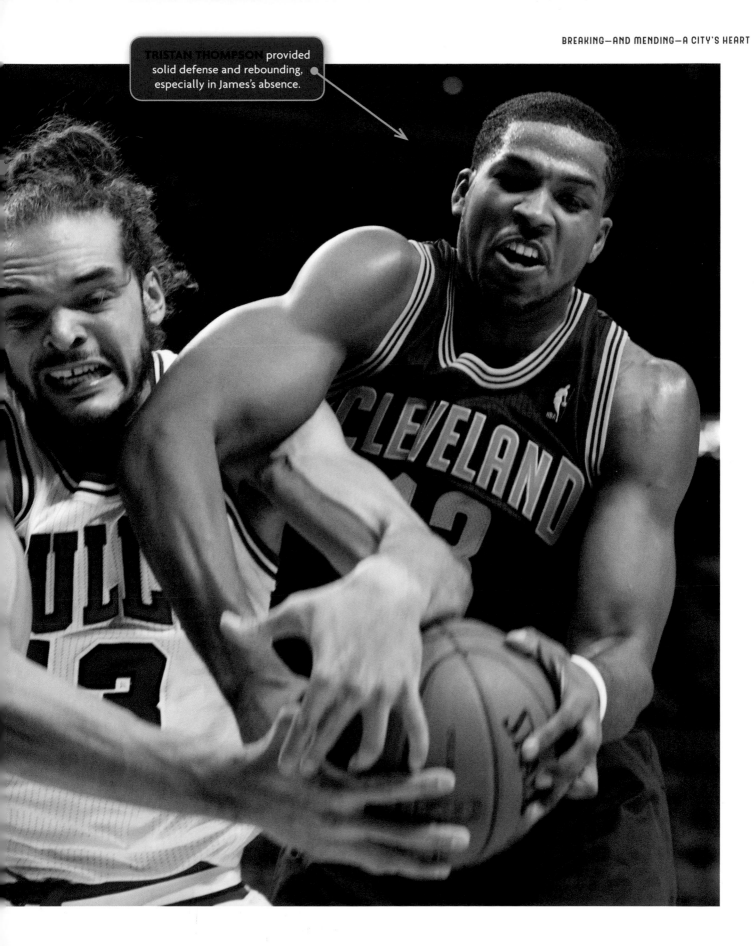

TRISTAN THOMPSON provided solid defense and rebounding, especially in James's absence.

Big man **KEVIN LOVE** helped the Cavs defeat the Warriors in the 2016 NBA Finals.

An elite guard, **KYRIE IRVING** displayed smart leadership on the court.

Though the Cavs finished just behind Boston in the Eastern Conference in 2016–17, they made it through the first three rounds of the playoffs with only one loss. They faced Golden State for the third year in a row in the Finals. James became the first player in NBA history to average a triple-double in the Finals. He also surpassed Michael Jordan to become the all-time playoffs scoring leader. But there would be no miracle finish for Cleveland that year. The Cavs won just one game.

Cleveland fans loyally supported the Cavs through all their ups and downs. They rejoiced when native son LeBron James led the team to its first-ever NBA title. They look forward to more championship banners hanging inside Quicken Loans Arena very soon.

SELECTED BIBLIOGRAPHY

Ballard, Chris. *The Art of a Beautiful Game: The Thinking Fan's Tour of the NBA.* New York: Simon & Schuster, 2010.

Hubbard, Jan, ed. *The Official NBA Basketball Encyclopedia.* 3rd edition. New York: Doubleday, 2000.

McKee, Vincent. *The Cleveland Cavaliers: A History of the Wine and Gold.* Charleston, S.C.: Arcadia, 2014.

NBA.com. "Cleveland Cavaliers." http://www.nba.com /cavaliers/.

Simmons, Bill. *The Book of Basketball: The NBA According to the Sports Guy.* New York: Ballantine, 2009.

Sports Illustrated. *Sports Illustrated Basketball's Greatest.* New York: Sports Illustrated, 2014.

46

WEBSITES

DUCKSTERS BASKETBALL: NBA
http://www.ducksters.com/sports/national_basketball_association.php

Learn more about NBA history, rules, positions, strategy, drills, and other topics.

JR. NBA
http://jr.nba.com/

This kids site has games, videos, game results, team and player information, statistics, and more.

Note: Every effort has been made to ensure that any websites listed above were active at the time of publication. However, because of the nature of the Internet, it is impossible to guarantee that these sites will remain active indefinitely or that their contents will not be altered.

INDEX